HEALING FROM MYSELF

Sometimes the Best Thing You Can Do for Yourself is to Let Go

Lotoya Francis

Hasmark PUBLISHING INTERNATIONAL

Published by
Hasmark Publishing International
www.hasmarkpublishing.com

Editor: Jamie Geidel jamie.geidel@gmail.com
Cover Design: Anne Karklins anne@hasmarkpublishing.com
Interior Layout: Amit Dey amit@hasmarkpublishing.com

ISBN 13: 978-1-77482-178-7
ISBN 10: 1774821788

TABLE OF CONTENTS

PREFACE

This book is dedicated to all truth seekers and those who long to discover a better world. In the process of writing this book, I too was in a world of dismay, covered by toxic thoughts that forced me to settle for unsatisfying situations. For years I thought that the key to happiness was outside of me and someone else possessed the key. It was not until I embarked on my healing and spiritual journey that I discovered I did not need to heal from anyone—I needed to heal from myself. I had settled for jobs, partnerships, and relationships that neither satisfied nor nourished my soul. I unknowingly self-sabotaged and I placed myself in situations that were not serving me or deserving of my energy. It took time to get on this path of knowing and becoming. In healing, I began to understand that I am the creator of my worlds and experiences, and if I wanted to enhance the experiences that I was having in life, I needed to start with *me*.

CHAPTER 1

REMOVING THE LITTER: FINDING YOUR *WHY*

The moment you decide to change your path, life will ask you, "Why?" Life will bring you to various tests, but throughout you must stay true to your *why*. To change your life, you first need to understand yourself and find out "Why were you created?"And if you have found the answer to that question, then "Why aren't you living within your full self? "

For years I held on to things that were not serving to me because of fear. I did not want to come off to others as "too much." I feared that if I stood out I would not be liked; I didn't want to offend anyone. I suppose that this belief developed from what happened to me as a child.

I was five years old. My school principal, Mrs. Skyers, appointed me to be the leader for my class graduation. I was so excited to have been chosen and practiced for weeks, perfecting my voice as well as my dance moves. I felt so honored to have been chosen by my school principal. But on the day of graduation, rather than being met with support from the other parents, I was met with bitterness. The sharp stares and scoffs turned my excited mood into fear and sadness. The other parents were upset that I had been chosen to lead the graduation. I remember midway through I had asked my school teacher to please let me go last; I didn't want to offend anyone.

It's amazing the things that stand out from our childhood, the traits we unwilling accept, and the beliefs that stay with us because of unsatisfying situations. That memory stayed with me for years. Each time I was given an opportunity to evolve, I subconsciously blocked it because I was holding onto the fear of offending. For years I held onto the quote that my five-year-old self whispered—"Let me go last." And for years I held onto that thought subconsciously—*Let me go last.*

It took me years to find out that this was the reason I held myself back. Knowing this, I was able to change my thought and replace it with one of confidence and pride, but it was not easy. I embarked on a healing journey that sometimes left me feeling lonely, scared, and heartbroken. Over the years I came to understand that if I wanted to grow in the way that aligned with the vision that I have of self, I needed to let go of those toxic beliefs and people that I had gravitated to over the years. Coming to this realization was not easy. I battled with it. I battled with staying in my comfort zone versus the image I saw within. I knew I wanted to become more, but I was afraid of stepping into my truth.

The fact is that as humans, we often resist change because of fear of the unknown. Holding onto this fear will only restrict your growth and stifle your authenticity. My healing journey led me to understand that I am much more than my physical experience. I am not the broken child that needed validation on the day of her graduation. I am not the single mom who struggled to parent a toddler. I am a spiritual being having a human experience. Knowing this gave me the confidence to own my truth, and my truth is anything that I want it to be.

Over the years I had become used to doing things in a specific way. At first, dreaming of more and going after it sometimes left me feeling extremely anxious. The thing about the mind is that once it becomes comfortable with a specific routine, it will reject change; change makes it uncomfortable. For years I went back and forth with the thought of pursuing a better way, or staying in the same spot. Knowing your worth and being afraid to stand in that light is a very hard place to be. I searched for the right method of getting on the right path. That is when I discovered *The Secret. The Secret* was a DVD that came out, talking about the universal law of attraction. This was my introduction to the metaphysical teachings of the universe. I was excited to have stumbled upon such knowledge, and I needed to know more, so I dug deeper. This is when I was introduced to the works of Neville Goddard and Joseph Murphy, who are teachers of metaphysics. They taught me the law of abundance and peace. Neville spoke about the law of attraction like no other. He spoke in a way that my soul identified with, and this led me to discover my truth. I began seeing the path much clearer. I saw myself as a powerful being. This gave me confidence to claim my true identity.

The more in tune I got with the law, the more I started to understand that to change my reality, I needed to master my thoughts. For years I found myself in a pattern of being motivated, then letting go when I was met with a challenge within. Normally I would fall back into the pattern of resorting to unsatisfying beliefs of self and being consumed in bad experiences. I started to understand that if I wanted change, I must reconstruct my mind, I must be ready to let go of my old self and be renewed with the new me.

I started to be more conscious about the types of conversations I was engaging in. I no longer talked about lack or held onto unsatisfying desires. When I started to become aware of my thoughts, I was amazed by the thoughts I engaged in; I felt ashamed to know that I had allowed those thoughts to rule my life.

I began to realize that to truly grow, I needed to uproot all that no longer served me. This meant truly letting go of the old self and rebuilding my life in the way that I envisioned it within.

CHAPTER 2

IDENTITY MARKERS

An identity marker is a memory that creates a blueprint in your personality, most times associated with trauma. Something happens, and from that negative experience you form an identity.

This particular scene in your memory constantly shows up to remind you, sometimes at the most inconvenient times. The identity marker stems from a place, an event, a fear, and that one memory defines who you are. It took me years to understand that my identity marker was that five-year-old kid who feared not being liked and as a result, self-sabotaged. This little girl showed up in my relationships, jobs, and quality of life.

Understanding your identity marker is the easiest part. Disengaging from that thought and belief pattern will be one of the most challenging things you will ever do. I needed to give birth to a new identity, but first I needed to heal—heal from my thoughts and old belief patterns.

Sometimes the best thing you can do for yourself is to let go—let go of the need to be right, the need to be validated or appreciated. For a while I held on to the thoughts that my five-year-old self echoed—"Don't stand out; it's too much attention." Having this thought and discovering that my aligned path is to be a life coach and motivational speaker scared me. How can I be all these things if I am "shy"? At least that's what I told myself to get out of anything that was considered to be out of the norm. For years this is the story I told myself. Recognizing your identity markers will aid in your self-development. It will allow you to identify when you are thinking from a place of fear and will help you to push beyond those fearful thoughts.

Now that you have identified your identity markers, how do you heal? This is a question I ask myself daily. *How do I move from this? How do I become better? The tiredness that comes with feeling stuck can be overwhelming. Now that I know who I am, how do I show up as she?* I hear a voice echo in my heart—"Change." Sounds simple, right? Those of you who have invested time into real change will know that it doesn't happen overnight. There are days when you feel that you are doing all the right things, only to be brought back to a place of fear and trying to find comfort in what you knew. Some days I feel like I am on top of the world and that I can accomplish anything; then there are those days when I feel I am drowning in my own pain and feeling mentally and physically exhausted, feeling too tired to fight my way out.

There was a particular time when I felt overwhelmed. It was different from all the other times. I was a single mom parenting a toddler, living in a one-bedroom apartment and feeling tired—not just physically tired, but emotionally drained. I remember saying to myself, "I am not her anymore, I can't be her anymore." The "her" that I was referring to was my five-year-old self who was founded through fear. I started to despise her and everything she stood for. She was the reason my life was the way that it was, and I wanted no part in harboring her failing beliefs. From that day forward I decided to reframe my life, by not allowing my identity markers to define me.

I remember throughout high school, I was the shy girl. I remember during our school assembly wanting to get up out to the audience and say something on stage. I had an urge for my voice to be heard, but sadly that little voice of my five-year-old self always seemed to overpower me; fear would set in, fear of what others would think, or say. Discovering my spiritual self helped me to recognize my power. I didn't have to hold onto disempowering thoughts or beliefs. My spirituality gave me the urge to evolve, and I did. I started listening to and trusting the voice within. This was the start of my journey into self. I learned ways about myself that I would have otherwise denied. I was the cause of all this. I needed a change. I longed to discover a different identity—one that was not founded by "her".

CHAPTER 3

GROUNDWORK: PLANTING SEEDS

Identifying my personality traits helped me to know and learn about myself a bit more. Of course, I know myself in the physical form. I am talking about truly knowing myself in the spiritual part of it. I jumped many hurdles, fought a long hard battle, and endured emotional trauma, but I have arrived to this place, a higher expression of self.

Let's talk about how I began to plant my seeds. A few years ago I went on a quest to discover myself. I wanted to heal. I was tired of carrying around the pain from past trauma; I no longer wanted to live there. Holding onto pain can cause you to experience grief daily. Pain often tries to have a permanent place in your life. By reliving painful experiences you will be kept in mental anguish. If you choose to carry each experience along with you, it will be very hard to differentiate who you are from what happened to you. I know some people who have built their lives upon a trauma-based experience. They are afraid to get out of it because it is all they know, and they are unaware of how to set themselves apart from what and who broke them.

For a while I introduced myself as what broke me and threw myself various pity parties, often attended by family and friends. I didn't know how to disassociate myself from that trauma. It is when I started incorporating the metaphysical teachings into my Christian beliefs that I began merging into the true possibilities of life.

How many of you still live in your trauma? How many times have you attempted to emancipate yourself from toxic thoughts?

It can be done. The truth is that you will never have everything all figured out perfectly, and you will constantly be learning and growing. But I have learned that you can steer your life in the path you need and want. The key is to manage what gets into your mind. You can never stop yourself completely from having bad thoughts, but the key is that the moment you start thinking negatively, replace that thought with a positive one. I never thought that I would be able to gain this skill, but I did. Through this process, I discovered my true self.

There are days that I just want to snap and tell someone who has offended me where to go, but lately I am able to think and recall much more quickly that arguing and fighting are tools that soothe the ego, that make the ego feel important. How you carry yourself and the standard that you hold for yourself is all you need. There will be people who come around to disrupt your vibe and flow. You fall victim the moment you let their turmoil get inside your sacred space.

Discovering God has been one of the most life-changing experiences, but when I say God I don't mean someone outside of you. I mean the God who lives within. Your soul is your highest connection to source. The human part of us has humanized God. We place a color, height, and gender on God. We limit our understanding of God by conforming God to just the physical experience. We are spiritual beings having a human experience. The moment you are able to separate your physical experience from your spiritual, you will be one step closer to discovering your truest expression of self.

For a while, I too held a limited experience of God, and I formed God in the physical realm. But you see, pain is the teacher that gives you a sense of redirection. Through my pain and hurt I was motivated to dig deep into metaphysical teachings. There I found out that heaven was within me and that by being truthful to myself and nurturing myself both physically and spiritually, I would get to create and recreate heaven each day.

I don't know what happened; I believe that something shifted within the universe. I began to be exposed to some sacred knowledge and information about metaphysics. It is said that when the student is ready, the teacher will appear, and that is what happened to me. Before I discovered Neville's teaching, I was depressed and struggled with self-image. I was confined to thoughts of lack and fear. I lived in a world that I felt was handed to me. I knew I needed to make a change, and discovering Neville's work helped me to do that. I was in a time and space where I was ready to evolve. I figured, why not? Why not change thoughts and liberate myself of the toxic thoughts that have held me back for years? I find it interesting how Neville related most of his teaching to the Bible. This gave me the option to explore the Bible much more intensely and for the first time understand it much more in depth.

I believe that spirituality is a liberation of self. It gives you the freedom to explore without confinement. It also gives you great knowledge and understanding of your true self, while embracing you in a nonjudgmental zone.

How will you be able to discover your most authentic self? In order for me to walk within my truth, I needed to do the necessary groundwork, which was understanding why I needed a change and what I was willing to sacrifice in order to achieve the desired state. I needed a change because I no longer wished to be confined to the reality of my old self. I believed in my worthiness and was ready to walk within my truth. I was willing to sacrifice self—the old self, the old beliefs, the old thought patterns that had held me down for years.

We all have greatness within us, and we all possess the tools to become the best version of ourselves. There just has to be a moment when you say, "This is enough. I want a change," and consistently work on yourself for that change to come to fruition. The reason that many fail is because they have refused to do the groundwork that is needed to make themselves better. They get too comfortable in the story that they have imagined for themselves. Change seems like a lot of work, but it is one of the most rewarding experiences you will have.

Sometimes this means rooting out all that does not serve you. This means working on your toxic traits and dedicating yourself to living a better and more fulfilled life, letting go of people and an environment that does not fit your new identity. When you let go and allow your higher self to speak and take over, your ancestors rejoice because this means that one more soul has found the road to self-discovery. You discover the voice of divine energy, and it will speak to you on the days you feel alone and afraid. It will remind you that you are on the right path and will guide you when you have lost your way. The more you begin to trust this voice, the more you begin to trust yourself. You will never be a perfect master of self, but the more healing you have done, the more understanding you will be of your triggers and the better you will be able to control them. Knowing that we are much more than our physical form living in this physical world, you become closer to your emancipation of the physical world and closer to discovering the spiritual reality.

The moment when I refused to allow past failures or bad experiences to define me was the moment I started setting standards for my experiences. I consciously chose to work on the areas of myself that needed me to show up. That means speaking up when I had something to say and unapologetically walking in my truth. When I chose to silence my fears, I silenced my five-year-old self and gently reminded her that she was no longer in charge.

It is important to understand that your shadow personality that had clinged to you for years is very much a part of your *now* as she was a part of your past. This personality over the years unintentionally developed ways of protecting you. These ways were developed through fear. The shadow tries to protect you from repeating past experiences by reminding you of pain. It is important to gently disassociate yourself from this part of your identity. Whenever you are being triggered, remind yourself, "This experience is only for a moment. It will not define me."

People often ask me how I knew when I was ready to refresh my life. My answer is this: when I accepted the fact that I needed healing. I was ready to let go; I had reached a point in my life when I stood up to life and decided I needed to change my story.

I learned to differentiate my true voice from the shadow voice and started to trust my inner voice. I stopped overthinking and chose not to play roles that I knew did not align with my purpose. By listening to my intuitive voice, the universe liberated me and rewarded me with purpose.

Discovering my spirituality led me closer to my higher self. It allowed me to explore different parts of myself through meditation and listening to vibrational frequencies. For the first time, I felt I was in control of both my physical and spiritual experience. The voice within that had been silent for so many years began to emerge. She was bold and confident, and she was ready to be heard.

I started taking chances that would normally scare me. I was speaking at events and helped motivate other women who were struggling to find purpose. Through helping them I began to heal myself.

One of the things I started doing towards my self-development was getting up at 5:00 a.m. every morning. That was the time I dedicated to myself. I got a head start to create my day. During my 5:00 a.m. routine I began to reflect on how I would want my day to be. I started to think from a place that was limitless.

I no longer chose to identify myself as a single mom who struggled to parent a toddler. I was a mom doing the best that she could with the tools she was given. I reframed my situation, and that helped changed my perspective. You have to change the narrative—then your reality will change. It is said that the power of life and death is within your tongue. Make sure that you speak greatness in the midst of your experiences. The moment when I refused to be the Lotoya that trauma created, I started having a better mental outlook on my life. I am the victor, not the victim. I deserve the best.

Living a purposeful life can be exhausting. I decided If I was going to be exhausted, it would be because I was giving life all I had, while maintaining a good balance and becoming the best version of me. I knew that if my current reality did not reflect what I wanted, I had the power to change it. This means not dwelling on what's happening on the outside, but rather focusing on the world inside and through those thoughts manifest my reality. Manifesting and believing is one of the hardest parts, but once you get in the groove of things it gets easier.

It is important to take time to plant your seeds. Laying your foundation is extremely important in your self-development. This will help you to remove the blockages when you meet resistance from the old self.

Get a notebook and write down your goals. There is power in the pen. When I was going through a rut at one point in my life, I remember all I used to do was journal. I wrote my goals down and was eager and motivated when I was able to cross them off as I accomplished them.

The old self will cling to what feels safe and will fight you when it realizes that you are doing something that contradicts the identity that was formed through fear and trauma. It will try to remind you that it is uncomfortable by forcing you to relive moments that caused you pain. This is a ploy to distract you from the bigger picture. You must work through this. Once you do, the old self becomes less powerful.

I realize that you will never be a perfect master of self, but you can be a ruler of self-limiting thoughts by choosing to shut them down and replacing a negative thought with a positive one.

Molding your ground and getting the groundwork ready for planting seeds means letting go of any and every thing that no longer serves you. This means relationships that were formed from the identity of the old self. It means removing self-limiting beliefs. It means recreating yourself to match the feeling within. When I look back at where I was mentally a few year ago, I am amazed by my growth. The more evolved I became, the less I identified with my former self, and the more empowered I felt. For years I was afraid to try, afraid of my own potential, and I allowed other people's ideas and beliefs to govern who I was. This came in the form of friends and partners. I feared standing out. This meant settling for less because of the belief that if I desired more it would attract too much attention. I used to be "her", and I am thankful to have given birth to my new self, one that is bold and confident. I am thankful to have found my voice. I am thankful to have given birth to the real me.

Planting seeds is not all about your inner work. It means helping others to plan and recognize their own harvest. People ask me about my journey, how I knew that I wanted to be a life coach and motivational speaker. I tell them that it just happened. It was not something I had thought about doing. Given my background, this would not have been my first career choice, but everything is divinely planned, and this path was laid out for me long before I was a thought in my mother's eyes. Through my healing I discovered myself, and by discovering myself I discovered my purpose.

I found that the more I walked into my truth, my mental health just naturally started to feel better. The peace that comes with walking in your truth is incredible. It is said that you know what is good for your soul by how it makes you feel within. On this path I feel free. I am liberated because I have discovered my "I am-ness" and I am walking in my unfiltered truth. You are always learning and growing. Life will try to mold you through experiences, and oftentimes those experiences are made to set us on the right path, regardless of how painful it might feel at the time. Long ago I felt that the universe was working against me, but through my spirituality I learned that it was working to help me discover my truest expression of self.

CHAPTER 4

SHADOW WORK

Let me tell you about your shadow! It took me some time to get down this road to self-healing and discovery. Now I understand why it took me so long to get here. I needed to work on my shadow. The shadow is a part of you that was created by a bitter experience in your childhood. Oftentimes we become products of our environment, collecting identical traits to those of our caregivers. As a result we carry their traits and form them into our own identity. Sometimes this causes us to have self-limiting beliefs that are carried into our adult life. It plays out in our choices of partners and how we govern our emotions. It took me years to find that my shadow was five-year-old Lotoya who was born the day of her kindergarten graduation. This shadow follows me everywhere in my jobs, my choices of partners, and my career path.

It took a lot of self-work to realize that I was the cause of many of my life experiences. This was because of my tendency to self-sabotage.

You often hear healers talk about shadow work. The shadow part of you represents your insecurities and fears. It shows up at various times in your life. For me, my shadow showed up when I was stepping out of my comfort zone. The five-year-old me would show up to remind me that I would be seen, and she doesn't like to be seen. For years I felt I was at war with myself. It was the me who needed change versus the me who was uncomfortable to move forward. I learned that to change I needed to stop fighting with my shadow. I needed to try to understand my shadow, and by understanding her, I would eventually break myself away.

I was up for a promotion at work. I remember going home that night feeling elated that I was being considered. I went about preparing myself mentally for the task ahead. It started with a prayer of gratitude for the new season that I was stepping into followed by a deep meditation. I turned on my solfeggio frequency 528hz[1] and started to meditate. Deep within my meditative state, my five-year-old self appeared to me. She had a look of fear on her face. The mind started to wonder, thoughts arose. *What if I fail? What if they laugh?*

I instantly replaced the fear with empowering thoughts. I started imagining myself growing in power and becoming the best, finding my self-worth and truly living my truth. My thoughts started to become silent, and for the first time I felt separated from my five-year-old self. I no longer could

---

[1] According to https://www.bettersleep.com/blog/science-behind-solfeggio-frequencies/ "Solfeggio frequencies refer to specific tones of sound that help with and promote various aspects of body and mind health. These frequencies . . . date back to ancient history and [are] said to be the fundamental sounds used in both Western Christianity and Eastern Indian religions . . . Physician and researcher, Dr. Joseph Puleo, rediscovered Solfeggio frequencies in the 1970s, bringing their benefits back into public awareness . . . he used mathematical numeral reduction to identify six measurable tones that bring the body back into balance and aid in healing."

identify myself with her. Her fears were no longer my own. Her thoughts were no longer my own. We lived in two different worlds, and I no longer wanted her to be a part of mine. My five-year-old self appeared to be very scared, locked into fear. I felt the urge to embrace her. Suddenly I uttered the words, "I am okay!" In this moment I recognized that I did not need to fear my truth. I thanked her for protecting me, and I told her that it was okay for me to do it on my own now. I felt as if a ton of bricks had been lifted from my back. This was the first time that I have ever experienced this level of consciousness during my meditative state. I felt an intense sense of empowerment, control, and clarity.

We often look outside of ourselves for change when we should be looking in the mirror. I suppose it is easier said than done. We are so used to giving and empowering everything outside of ourselves. Healing is a journey and not a sprint. Sometimes you feel you have healed and evolved from a particular situation only to be reminded that you have yet to begin the healing process. The healing journey is sometimes a painful and frustrating journey. It will have you in a state of feeling peaceful, anxious, and happy all at once. Sometimes I would think to myself, *Am I doing it right?* But then I realized that everyone's journey is different, and unfortunately no one has a cheat sheet to life, so I started to take it easy on myself. We are all trying to figure out our journey, which is uniquely packaged for each of us. We are all trying to be the best version of ourselves while deprogramming from our old selves and reprogramming with new empowering thoughts and ways.

After the encounter with my five-year-old self, I realized that things started to just naturally work in my favor. I had let go of the self-limiting beliefs that plagued my mind for years. By doing this, I gave birth to my highest self. Who am I? I am Lotoya Francis, life coach and motivational speaker. I am going to show up as she every day. On the days that I am tired I will remain steadfast in my identity; on the days I experience unsatisfying situations, I will remain true to her. There are days that my five-year-old self shows up, sometimes just before I make an important decision; however her voice is not as loud, her impact not as powerful. Whenever she shows up, I gently remind her that I am ok, that she does not need to protect me, and that I am comfortable in the space I am in.

Discovering my voice has really granted me amazing opportunities that have led me to discover and experience a different part of my consciousness. Neville Goddard said in one of his lectures, "You must put away the old man and be renewed by the new." My rebirth happened the moment I took control over my life. I sometimes identify my previous life as a prison because that is exactly how it felt. I was caved into thoughts that oftentimes manipulated and lowered my vibration. I got tired, and by getting tired of how I was allowing my thoughts to rule my life, I ultimately changed my entire perception of the physical and spiritual world. I would advise anyone who is going through their healing journey to get to know your shadow and start from there.

CHAPTER 5

BE "DELUSIONAL"

I suppose some would call me delusional. After all, anyone who chooses not to believe in what the masses think . . . is somewhat crazy, right? When I talk about frequencies and vibrations and listening to decades-old lectures, it is not the taste that many people acquire, but for me it feels like heaven. Listening to lectures on metaphysical teaching and meditating is the combo for the gods.

Do you know how powerful we are? You are a powerful being that lowered your vibration by entering into the human form. Some would say it is a sacrifice you made of self, knowing that the physical world will try to limit your vibration by programming you to have limitations, knowing you will not be taught to empower your spiritual self, knowing you will need to embark on that journey alone. The more in tune you are with your spirituality, the more you will understand that the only limitation is what you create within your mind.

We are limitless beings, but we have been brainwashed into thinking that what we see in physical reality is all that there is, all that exists. And we neglect to acknowledge that everything in the physical world had to first be created in the spiritual world, in people's minds and limitless imagination, before it took physical form.

You and you alone are responsible for the thoughts that you carry within your mind. If you want to achieve greatness, the moment you claim it and have a definite purpose in achieving it, the universe will provide you with people along the way who will help you to achieve your worthy idea.

The moment you discover your highest self, you must walk within your truth. It must be an obsession. You must walk in it morning, noon, and night. It doesn't matter what anyone else says. You must walk in your truth until it manifests into physical reality. This is how true change occurs.

Once you acquire knowledge of the metaphysical teachings, you must be mindful of who and what gets into your circle of light. You must guard your place of peace because it is where you will find solitude on the days you need inspiration.

I became obsessed when it came to my goals. I knew that to define what I wanted and to achieve it, I had to dive into limitless possibilities almost to the point of being what some people would call "delusional". I had to blind myself to everything that did not align with my vision. At the time I was living in a one-bedroom apartment that I shared with my toddler. At the time, I needed more space. I did not want to move to another apartment; the vision was to own my own home.

I knew I needed to be "delusional" the moment I discovered metaphysics, and now I was determined to put the law to the test. I pictured what my new home would look like, and I slept in the assumption every night that I was there until it manifested in physical reality. I didn't ask for anyone's approval; I did not care how the housing market looked. I wanted what I wanted, and I was ready to live it everyday. Every night before I went to sleep, I slept as I would sleep had I been in my dream home. I imagined everything lifelike in detail—how the bed would feel, how the sheets would feel on my body, the light in the bedroom, was it dark? My curtains and walls, how my feet felt when they touched the ground of my bedroom floor. I lived in my dream house in the moment, and soon it manifested.

I tell my clients to never be afraid. There is no limit to who you can be; there is no limit on greatness. Have high standards and exquisite taste. Most days I am my own cheerleader and biggest supporter. I like it this way; this way I will always be fueled by my own belief. Any other support anyone adds is just a bonus.

For years I battled with my self-identity. At some stages I was too skinny, at other stages I was too fat, too tall, not pretty enough. Looking back at all those crippling beliefs about myself held me in a dark cage that only I had the key to. I was now on a mission to do everything that made my old self uncomfortable. I started nurturing my beliefs by being totally oblivious to my physical reality, and I began to invest in myself. I started my podcast, the *Coaching Life Podcast*. I talked about the teachings that liberated me from the web that entangled me for years. I started doing mirror techniques. This is speaking to your reflection as the man or woman you want to be. I oftentimes stand in the mirror and speak to my reflection. I used to imagine that I was speaking in front of thousands of people, helping and motivating them to become the best version of themselves.

I was she, Lotoya Francis, life coach and motivational speaker. I discovered my truth, and no one could tell me otherwise.

One day I was home, and I got a call. They wanted me to speak at a charity event that empowers women who were coming out of abusive situations. I thought to myself, *this is it! You have opened the portal, and you have to keep going.* I went and spoke and dropped a lot of gems. I left that event feeling powerful and motivated.

I realized that the seeds that I have planted were now springing forth. And I needed to continue to walk in the faith I planted within. I started taking on more public speaking gigs that allowed me to use my voice as well as empower other women and men who were looking to break away from their former identities. The more I began to embrace this side of myself, the better I felt within. I decided to let go of playing it safe and to embrace myself in my truest and most authentic form. We are learning in this physical experience, but the more connected you are to who you are within, the easier it gets.

CHAPTER 6

BROKEN MIRRORS

The birth of all new experiences comes from your broken mirror. How many of us are walking around with broken mirrors? For years I walked around with a broken mirror which was tainted through the lens of bad experiences. Sometimes we don't recognize our broken mirrors until the memories of our bad experiences cut us so deep, we start bleeding on other people.

We are living in a society that glorifies perfection, looking good on the outside while bleeding from the brokenness we feel inside. I didn't know I was broken. I thought I was healed. I thought I was okay and that I was not to blame for what was happening in my life; it was they, them, and everything else to blame. It was not until I started my healing that I recognized *I* was responsible for what was happening to me. I took ownership of the role I played in what went wrong in my life, but it wasn't easy.

One of the hardest tasks you can take on is parenting a child while trying to repair your own broken mirror. No one talks about the struggles that you will sometimes face while healing yourself and trying to raise an unbroken human. One of the hardest things I had to do was to parent while healing. As a parent you want to be the best parent. You want to be able to raise your children to be productive and healthy individuals. But sometimes when you are on your own healing journey, it can get a bit challenging. I have learned not to be too hard on myself and drew close to the saying that goes, "Even on your best days you will feel like you are not good enough." Finding a healthy foundation you can stand on to be a productive parent is what will help you on those weary days.

I was around twenty-eight when I realized that I no longer wanted to feel broken. I was tired, mentally and physically overwhelmed, tired of allowing my thoughts to overpower me, ready to evolve. I had lived my life one way, through the old identity, and I was now ready to live how I wanted, that is, being free both physically and spiritually. I began to repair my broken mirror. I started looking in the mirror more often, I mean really looking within, far from the physical part of me, rather from the power that fuels this physical being. The more I looked within, the more I began to form a new identity and gather newfound respect and admiration for myself. I started to show appreciation for my body. It has kept me for so long and carried me through much pain and many disappointments after all the experience and fight I had put into this life. This is the body I have. I started appreciating my body and myself and got back into doing things that felt good to me, spending more time getting to know myself, my likes and dislikes, and really paying attention to myself. I started taking care of my mind by removing a lot of toxic thinking I had; I replenished it with thoughts of peace and acceptance of self.

We sometimes get so caught up in taking care of others, we forget about taking care of ourselves. I was truly learning about myself for the first time—broken but still strong, afraid but ready to thrive.

The truth is that your broken mirror will never leave you. It will stay with you forever. No matter how you have healed, you will always remember what broke you and how it made you feel. Regardless of your willingness to let go, you will always be reminded. I have learned to not be afraid of my broken mirror, I have learned to embrace it and learn from and through it.

CHAPTER 7

READY NOW?
WALK THE WALK!

Once you come to the self-realization that you are the creator of your own experiences, you become much stronger. Letting go and walking in your truth is one of the hardest things you can do. I remember when I was called to do motivational speaking. I thought, *how can I possibly be "she"?* But I made a promise to myself, that no matter how hard it gets, never give up. Even when the doors took a while to open, I had to be "she" and that means walking by faith. That means believing in myself and getting over the need for validation. I was she, Lotoya Francis, life coach and motivational speaker. I was ready to walk the walk.

I started to learn to calm down my emotions and find what my triggers were. I started trying to understand what my self-limiting beliefs were and began to work on them. I needed to evolve and experience a different, more aligned physical reality. By learning about myself, I was that much closer to becoming "she". I am somewhat of a deep thinker, sometimes imagining the worst-case scenarios. When I started to do the self-work, I became more aware of my triggers and worked to understand them. By becoming aware of them, it got easier to silence them. I started dismissing anything and everything that did not align with the vison I had of self. I motivated myself by reminding myself that while I no longer was where I had been, I was certainly not yet where I wanted to be. Soon I manifested my first book; I started posting regularly on Tik Tock, building my followers and broadening my audiences.

It started getting really lonely. I was told that once you decide to make a real change, the road that one embarks on will not be easy. There were lots of bumps and bruises along the way, sleepless nights, and uncertainty, but from that came clarity, self-love, and appreciation. For the first time, I started to love myself.

During the writing of this book, I experienced various types of negative emotions, but I refused to allow my self-limiting beliefs to stifle this project. I oftentimes listened to one of my favorite Neville Goddard lectures in which he talks about how imagination creates reality. From this lecture I learned about the law of attraction as well as the law of assumption. Neville teaches us that we all have the ability to change our lives. This is through our thoughts and belief patterns. The moment you desire something you must feel that it is already within your possession. And even if the physical world denies it, if you stay true to your vision, eventually it will manifest into reality.

I think one of the issues is that no one told me the hard work that is required in order to get aligned with the vision and all the mental clutter that you need to get rid of. Sometimes it can feel exhausting. At times you might even feel hopeless. But as the great motivational speaker Les Brown once said, "It's not over until I win." And I need to win.

For years I felt that I was at a tug-of-war with myself, feeling one thing and accepting another. Writing this book has helped me to say what I mean and mean what I say, and that means standing firm in my truth, understanding who I am, and showing up as "she" every day.

CHAPTER 8

BETRAYING THE OLD SELF

Yesterday I said goodbye to the old version of me. I had to. I can no longer identify myself with her. To get to my truth I had to disassociate myself from the version of me that was created through trauma and pain. I no longer want to be defined by my experience. I no longer seek comfort in living in that realm that limited my ability to thrive. I have dreams of a better tomorrow, one where I am not riddled with emotions and unhealed wounds. I suppose without those wounds and pain I would not have been writing this book. At times I have to change my interpretation of what pain is. Pain is a teacher, a motivator, the fuel that allows you to discover your truth.

How do you continue when the odds seem stacked against you? No one from where I was believed in themselves to the point that they could control their reality. I am a woman who has been molded through experiences both good and bad. I guess the difference with me is that I choose not to allow the pain from the bad experiences to define me and absorb my life. I have friends who grew older but not wiser, friends who believed that their lives were limited, and they would not be able to evolve. Many have said that within the mind is our garden. You plant whatever you like. Abundance, love, and success is all yours for the taking. All these things are obtainable, but you have to change your mindset.

The day I chose to write this book I was in limbo in my old self. I am a first-time author. I never attempted to write a book before. What the heck was I thinking? I did not know any other authors personally, nor did I ever think that this would be the route I would choose. *Life coach* and *motivational speaker* seems to have a ring to it, but I wasn't caught up in the title. I wanted the feeling. In the book by Neville Goddard *Feeling Is the Secret*, Neville spoke about feeling the state you desire, regardless of what the physical reality affirms.

I sometimes thought *is this possible for me? Why have I been guided to this path?* I came to understand that I did not need to fight it anymore. I found more peace when I was less resistant to the calling. I found that everything just happened to work itself out. I lack nothing in this world of endless possibilities.

While writing this book I did not disclose any details about it to others. I have learned that outside influence can scatter your forces. Not everyone will see your vision. Plant your seed and nurture it; eventually others will see your manifestation in physical reality.

I realize that I am much calmer now. I am not in any rush. I am allowing my guides to lead me, and I am confident in trusting the process, waiting my turn, and appreciating the journey. Life comes with its many changes, but I believe that once I am consistent in my efforts in becoming better than I was yesterday, something amazing will blossom from the experience. Once you take a leap of faith and make a bold move, the universe always will assist you by giving you pleasant experiences that manifest by way of the people who come into your life.

A few years ago, my mindset was in limbo. I was at war with myself. I needed a change, but the old self did not want to let go of its position. I met an amazing entity who manifested in physical form. This person, whom I will refer to as Mr. S, showed me the parts of myself that I would otherwise turn a blind eye to. These are the toxic traits I held onto for comfort, such as my ability to overthink and overstress on the simplest situation. Through this experience I was able to form a light within me that glowed with happiness, peace, and abundance. Sometimes it takes the ones closest to us to shed light on the darkest places that we have within. This external experience was one of the sources that inspired me to manifest this book and in turn become the best version of myself.

No matter how strong we appear to be in physical form, sometimes our soul needs rejuvenation. We get so caught up in making sure we are physically fit, but how about being mentally healthy and stable? I aim to be both, and this is what prompted my healing journey.

I got tired of feeling tired. I had to do something about it. I have seen my mother and father become slaves to their minds, caught up in a web of impossibilities and fear, being scared to step out of their comfort zone and having a very unacceptable relationship with money. They thought themselves to be poor. It never dawned on them that they had the ability to change this mindset. This mindset crippled my great-grandparents and attempted to cripple me. *It stops with me*, I thought to myself. I was not going to allow those self-limiting beliefs to have their hold on my generation. I spoke greatness in my bones daily, and twice on the days that I felt overwhelmed. I knew it was only a matter of time before my manifestation would come to fruition. I have expanded my wings. My name echoes greatness. I believed it, and I live it each day.

I remember having a conversation with one of my siblings. She felt overwhelmed because her current relationship was overwhelming both physically and spiritually. I said to her, "The only problem here is you. You have forgotten who you are." Expecting that she would be resistant to my observations, she replied, "You are amazing." I felt that to the depths of my soul, not because I was being complimented by her but because I felt it for myself as well. Sometimes we don't feel great, but when you align yourself with greatness within, the physical realm has no choice but to yield and affirm how you feel about yourself.

It took me a while to get here. It took some bravery, but I am happy to have reached up to a place where I feel my truth. A friend asked me once, "What happened to you?" referring to how shy and timid I used to be. I said to her, "I woke up!"

Once I woke up, I could not fall back asleep. I often reflect on the days when I was silent and I had so much to say, yet I allowed fear of the unknown to hold me back from speaking my truth.

Well, now I am here, awakened to the laws of the universe, and I am eagerly ready to share. How many of you are still sleeping, sleeping on your truth, unable to see yourself in a better light because you have subconsciously placed yourselves in a mindset that bleeds insecurity, telling stories of how you failed, how broken and scared you are, not understanding that by affirming all these things with your thoughts you are confirming this in your future?

In Job 3:25 it says that "The thing I feared has overtaken me." If a farmer plants corn, he will surely reap corn. If we plant bad thoughts we will reap what we planted. Think of your mind as extremely fertile ground. If you choose, it can be the source of all the greatness you aspire to, but it can also be the source of your pain. Learning to use your mind will empower you beyond your wildest dreams.

CHAPTER 9

EVOLVING
FROM THE ILLUSION

Sometimes I feel that we all get so caught up with the image filters, likes, and seeking validation from others that have become the norm, so much that it has made us lose track of what really matters, which is our self-identity, our truest form of self, flaws and all.

I too get caught up with the unreal reality of social media, where everything and everyone seems perfect. The truth is we are all perfect. The key thing is to understand your own beauty, and understand that everyone's concept of beauty is different. Understanding and loving your own unique beauty is what will carry you on the days when no one provides you with validation.

Before I became a mother, I was in perfect shape. I went to the gym every day and maintained a healthy diet. I thought that physical perfection was all you needed. Becoming a mom and seeing the change in my body oftentimes left me feeling uncomfortable. Others started making comments such as "You have gotten very big" or "How come you have not lost the baby weight?" Of course, a smile and a joke along with the comment would ease the tension, but it forced me to think thoughts that did not align with how I wanted to feel.

As I struggled with recreating my image, I started internalizing the pain and questioned myself. Why wasn't I able to lose the weight? Why wasn't I as motivated as I was before? The truth is that we will never be perfect if we study from someone else's timeline. After learning to love my new body, only then was I able to make the changes that were needed to get back to a better and healthier me—for me.

How many of you are caught up in the illusion of perfection? What makes you perfect? These days we base perfection on looks. If someone looks good externally, they must be perfect, right? I see some of the people who are considered to be perfect by social media standards, and it turns out they are battling unspeakable pain from within. A lot of our family and friends suffer from high functioning depression, but you will never know because they don't fit society's idea of what depression looks like. A person with high-functioning depression is someone who does not fit the norm of what the stereotypical depressed person looks like. They hold down a job and have a clean appearance, but deep down they are battling with holding together their mental health. The reason a lot of people don't actively seek help is that they sometimes try to convince themselves that others see them as perfect, and that's all that matters.

Many of us think if we have the house, the cars, and the great body, that is all that is needed to be happy. I have seen people who have it all and are still not happy. Breaking yourself of these old ideologies and liberating yourself from the physical world will enable you to create true happiness. We need to pull away from the illusion that we have been so heavily caught up in, chasing perfection and peace without realizing that perfection and peace is within us. It cannot be bought or given to you; you create it.

I liberated myself from this lazy concept of physical perfection by going deep within myself, finding ways to create peace from within, and appreciating the fact that I am me, wonderfully created.

Life is what we make it, and we have a choice every day to make it better.

EPILOGUE

Writing this book was my therapy. I needed to show myself that I could make it happen. How many of you have started a project, and after you have started you became less and less motivated? This happened to me. I remember moments of not picking up my laptop for weeks, but I kept telling myself I had to do this. I was ready to change the narrative of my life from a lost and fearful little five-year-old to an author. I am a living example that all you need is to just want change, and it will certainly happen. All you need to do is decide that you can. You have the ability to rise and become a better you; isn't that amazing?

In the midst of writing this book, I questioned myself. Was it possible for me to do this? I quickly silenced those thoughts with gratitude, thankful to have been given this vision of writing. Knowing how to silence the voice of fear helped me to push through on the days that I was doubtful and couldn't see the vision. I remember thinking to myself, imagine if you get it done. As Neville Goddard would say, "Imagine the feeling of the wish fulfilled." I am here, I told myself I would get here, and I am happy I did.

I would like to thank everyone who believed in this project, everyone who saw the vision and kept supporting me along the journey. Thank you. And to that person who is in the midst of their own life situation and waiting to find a way to their peace, it is possible. It is possible for better. All you have to do is be ready to change. For years I talked a good talk, but it was not until I changed my mindset that I was able to change my life. Everything that you hope to accomplish is on the other side of fear. Most of the things that we worry about and give energy to are not worth it.

One of my biggest inspirations is having the need for more. Once you have that burning desire to accomplish something, the universe will make way for you to attract all the things you desire.

ABOUT THE AUTHOR

Lotoya Francis is a life coach and motivational speaker, who has developed a great fascination for spiritual teachings, in particular about the metaphysics and universal laws of attraction. She is the author of *Healing from Myself*, a mentor, a motivator, and a living example that one can manifest anything when thoughts are aligned to feelings.

www.ingramcontent.com/pod-product-compliance
Lightning Source LLC
Chambersburg PA
CBHW051011050726
47592CB00007B/2803